COUNTRY TOPICS

SPAIN

Catherine Chambers and Rachel Wright

Illustrated by John Shackell

WATTS BOOKS

LONDON • NEW YORK • SYDNEY

This symbol appears on some pages throughout this book. It indicates that adult supervision is advisable for that activity.

Watts Books
96 Leonard Street
London
EC2A 4RH

Franklin Watts Australia
14 Mars Road
Lane Cove
NSW 2006
Australia

UK ISBN: 0 7496 1109 X
10 9 8 7 6 5 4 3 2 1
Dewey Decimal Classification 946

Editor: Hazel Poole
Designer: Sally Boothroyd
Photography: Peter Millard
Artwork: John Shackell and Teri Gower
Picture research: Ambreen Husain,
Annabel Martin, Juliet Duff

A CIP Catalogue record for this book
is available from the British Library

Printed in the United Kingdom

CONTENTS

Introducing Spain

Spain is the second largest country in Western Europe covering an area of 504,782 square kilometres, and includes the Balearic and Canary Islands. Its capital is Madrid, positioned in the centre of the country. Spain has borders with France, Portugal and Gibraltar.

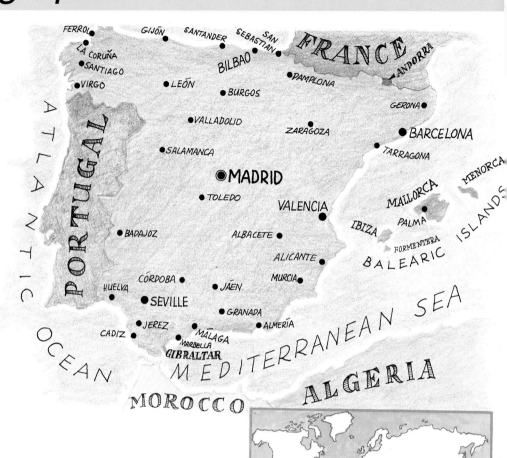

SPANISH STAMPS

Most Spanish stamps bear the head of King Juan Carlos, the present monarch. Each stamp has a single colour - some are bright pink or blue.

A special coin was minted in 1992 to mark the Barcelona Olympics.

MONEY, MONEY, MONEY

Spanish money is known as the peseta. The coins look like silver or brass and come in amounts of 1, 5, 10, 25, 50, 100, 200 and 500 pesetas. Notes are available for 1000, 2000, 5000 and 10,000 pesetas. They show the King on one side and a famous Spaniard on the other.

Old coins bear the head of Spain's previous ruler, General Francisco Franco, who died in 1975. These coins are being replaced by new ones showing the head of King Juan Carlos. A new five peseta coin has a design with no head at all on it.

HOW SPAIN IS RULED

The King of Spain is head of state and performs many official ceremonies. The Spanish government, the *Cortes,* is led by the prime minister. The *Cortes* is divided into two houses - the Congress of Deputies and the Council of Ministers.

Today's democratic system of governing has been in practice since 1975. Before that time, for 36 years, Spain was ruled by a dictator, General Franco.

SPANISH ANTHEM

The *Marcha Reál*, or Royal March, is the Spanish national anthem. It was brought to Spain in the 16th century by the Hapsburgs, the Austrian ruling family. No one knows who composed the anthem but, like the Spanish flag, it has lasted through many different kinds of government.

THE SPANISH FLAG

This bright, stripy flag has been flown as a symbol of Spain's unity since 1785. The red and yellow represent the ancient Catholic royal families of Castile and Léon. Over the years, this flag has altered very little.

CAR SPOTTING

You can tell which part of Spain a car comes from just by looking at its number plate. For example, this car came from Madrid. Here is a list of some others.

SA	Salamanca
B	Barcelona
MA	Malaga
BI	Bilbao
S	Seville

Say it in Spanish
la bandera - flag
el pais - country
la cocha - car
la oficina de correos - post office
el sello - stamp
el banco - bank
el dinero - money

5

Around Spain

Spain is a land of mountain and marsh, forest and desert, and a vast windy plain. It is one country, but it has 17 regions, four languages and a patchwork of different scenery and architecture.

Average temperatures		
Place	January	July
Madrid	5°C	25°C
Seville	10.5°C	29°C
Barcelona	8°C	23.5°C

CLIMATE AND COUNTRYSIDE

The first thing you feel as you travel around Spain is the change in climate. In the north, the Atlantic Ocean brings cold, stormy weather during the winter and warm, showery summers. Southern Spain faces the dry, blistering winds from North Africa, which are cooled by a small strip of Atlantic Ocean between Spain and Africa.

Eastern Spain is affected by the Mediterranean Sea. It brings mild, wet winters and hot, sometimes steamy, summers.

In the centre of Spain, the huge, high plateaus, known as the northern and southern Meseta, are blasted by hot, dry winds in the summer. But in the winter, it is bitterly cold and thick fog often covers the plains.

A warm, moist climate, and rich, volcanic soil have given the Canary Islands thick, tropical vegetation.

There are mountain ranges in the north and the south. Temperatures here vary greatly from snow on the mountainside to very hot sun at the bottom of the mountains. The Montes Universales, in the Valencia region, have snow for eight months of the year.

You may see some of Spain's wildlife in the many deserted parts of the country. Lynxes, wolves, wildcats, bears, wild boar and eagles are some of the creatures that roam freely.

Rich, green fields cover the land between Galicia and Catalonia. In the south, palm trees, orange orchards and olive groves line the coastal areas.

The Balearic Islands have a similar climate to Spain's mainland Mediterranean coast. The coast is dimpled by small coves and rocky inlets. Inland, eucalyptus bushes and wild thyme perfume the air.

CASTLES AND COLUMNS

Spain has more than 10,000 castles. A lot can be seen in the Castile-León and Castile-La Mancha regions. Roman bridges spread over Spain's seven wide rivers, and Roman aqueducts still bring water to hot, dry towns. There are thousands of churches, built and decorated in styles with lavish names such as *Churrigueresque*.

Dotted throughout much of Spain are the houses, offices and restaurants designed by Antonio Gaudí, a 19th century architect. And in Mérida, a town originally built as a retirement home for Roman soldiers, a modern architect has designed the enormous Museum for Roman Art.

LANGUAGE AND LAND

Spanish, or Castilian, is the main language spoken in Spain. But there are three other languages to be heard around the country - Catalan in Catalonia (north-east Spain), Basque in the Basque region and Galician in Galicia (north-west Spain). These regions also fly their own flags. The best known of these is the red, green and white flag of the Basques.

Say it in Spanish
el verano - summer
el invierno - winter
la lluvia - rain
el sol - sun
la playa - beach
la montaña - mountain
el lenguaje - language
el castillo - castle
la iglesia - church

Food and Drink

Spain's great range of foods has come from its varied climate, and the different peoples who have settled in Spain over the centuries.

FARMING AND FISHING

Spain grows most of the food it needs, from apples, cherries and chestnuts in the north, past the cereals of the central plains, to the oranges, olives, almonds and rice of the south.

Pigs roam freely in fields, munching their way through the acorns of the holm oak tree. Spaniards would not be without pigs, as pork is made into delicious spicy sausages.

Salted hams are hung up in shops and bars, sometimes for many years before they are bought.

Fresh fish is caught all around the Spanish coast and in the rivers. Eels are an expensive delicacy.

ESSENTIAL INGREDIENTS

Tomatoes, peppers, onions, garlic and saffron are ingredients that Spanish cooks would not be without. Saffron (right) was introduced by the Arabs and is cooked with meat or rice, added to a soup, or sprinkled raw on a salad.

EATING HABITS

Breakfast in Spain is early, as many people go to work at the crack of dawn. Lunch can last for two to three hours and can consist of several courses. The evening meal is very often not eaten until 10pm or 11pm.

Breakfast normally consists of toast, golden-fried *churros* (strips of dough), or bread sticks and pastries. This is washed down with hot chocolate, milk or coffee.

MENU

Cocido Madrileño - a delicious stew (Madrid)

Angulas a la Bilbaína - baby eels in garlic sauce (Basque region)

Escalivada - grilled peppers, eggplant, tomato and onion (Catalonia)

Paella a la Valenciana - a mixture of rice, rabbit, snails and broad beans (Valencia).

At lunch time and in the evenings, people eat out in cafés or restaurants. Many people also go to bars where they nibble at snacks called *tapas* which are laid out on the counter. On Sundays, Spanish families often pack a picnic.

Spain produces wine in every region and is one of the world's leading exporters of wine and sherry. In the north, though, cider is very popular. Some soft drinks that you may like to try are the fresh lemon drinks, the thick fruit juices and *horchata*, a sweet tiger-nut milk drink.

SHOPPING AND EATING OUT

In Spain you can buy food in vast, modern supermarkets, or small corner shops and stores. But most people like to shop in the open or covered markets. Here, they can buy fresh fruit and vegetables, country cheeses and sausages, and wild rabbits and game birds.

Shopping List
el pan - bread
la leche - milk
la fruta - fruit
las legumbres - vegetables
el azúcar - sugar
el pescado - fish
el queso - cheese
el café - coffee
el vino - wine
el jerez - sherry

Say it in Spanish
el supermercado - supermarket
la carnicería - butcher
la mantaquería - general grocery
el desayuno - breakfast
el almuerzo - lunch
la cena - supper
La panadería sells only bread.
   La pastelería sells cakes, biscuits and sweet breakfast rolls.
      La verdulería sells fruit and vegetables.

Sweets from Spain

If you have a very sweet tooth, then *turrón* is definitely the snack for you. *Turrón* is a kind of nougat, made from honey and almonds, which is traditionally eaten by the Spanish after their Christmas meal. There are many varieties of *turrón* in Spain. Some are soft, like marzipan, while others are hard and brittle. Shop-bought *turrón* is often named after the part of Spain in which it is made. The crunchy variety is known as *Turrón Alicante*. The softer sort is often marked *Turrón Jijona*.

YOU WILL NEED:

To make your own
Turrón Jijona...

Ask an adult to help you.

1. Line the china dish with rice paper and put it to one side.

2. Lightly toast the almonds and hazelnuts under a grill for a minute or two. Stir the nuts as they toast to stop them from burning.

3. Put the nuts into the food processor and chop them finely.

4. Check that your mixing bowl is perfectly dry. Then carefully separate the eggs and add the egg white to the bowl. Put the yolks into a separate bowl - they can be used later to make other dishes such as scrambled eggs.

5. Beat the egg whites with the whisk until they form stiff little peaks. Then add the nuts and stir.

6. Put the honey and sugar in the saucepan and bring them to the boil.

7. Turn the heat down to low. Add the nut mixture to the honey and sugar and stir *constantly* for 10 minutes to keep the mixture from burning.

8. Remove the mixture from the heat and spoon it into the dish. Using the half-lemon, level the top of the mixture and then leave it somewhere to cool.

9. When your *turrón* has set and is completely cold, you can either cut it into squares to eat, or you can chop it into small pieces and serve it on top of vanilla ice cream.

One variety of *turrón* is made with black dyed sugar. It is said that on the night of January 6th, the Three Kings from the Nativity story visit the homes of children who have behaved badly during the previous year and leave them some of this coal-like *turrón* as a present.

Spanish Life

WHERE PEOPLE LIVE

Over three quarters of the Spanish population live in cities, usually in apartments in tall buildings. In the countryside, families live in whitewashed clay or stone houses.

In mountain areas, the houses are of a tyrolean style. To the south, in Castile-Léon, you can see whole villages of rich red buildings made of earth, baked in the hot sun.

Old and new houses in Casares, Costa del Sol.

In the south, houses have thick walls and small windows to keep out the summer heat and the cool winter winds. The outside walls are whitewashed every year to reflect the hot sun.

Some people who live among the sandstone hills have houses carved out of them. The front of a cave house looks just like an ordinary one.

Cave houses in Guadix east of Granada.

EARLY MORNINGS

In the early morning, special traffic police control the lines of cars of people driving to work. There are several different police uniforms to look out for in Spain depending on the area. In the Basque region, for example, the police wear bright red berets.

TAKING A BREAK

Newspapers and magazines are sold from kiosks in the street. *El Pais* gives the latest news while magazines such as *¡hola!* provide the gossip. From other kiosks on the pavements, people sell lottery tickets which hundreds of thousands of Spaniards buy each day.

Over the last 10 years, television has become the most popular form of family entertainment in Spain. Game shows and variety shows are great favourites.

OFF TO SCHOOL

School starts at 8am and does not finish until 5pm, but there is a long break between 1pm and 3pm when many children go home for lunch.

Spanish education tries to prepare children for the modern world. Technology and computer studies are widely taught. At 16 years, a student can leave school, or go on to study technical subjects. Some go on to college or university.

In June, all the schools close for about 10 weeks for the long summer holiday.

Secondary School Timetable

por la mañana	
8 - 9	las matemáticas
9 - 10	el francés
10 - 11	la historia
12 - 1	la ciencia
1 - 3	el almuerzo
por la tarde	
3 - 4	el inglés
4 - 5	la educación física

WHAT PEOPLE DO

In Spain, the car industry employs more people than any other manufacturing industry. More and more people have moved to the towns and cities to find work, but along the coast many still work in the fishing industry, and Spain has one of the largest fishing fleets in Europe. In rural areas, farmers grow produce to sell abroad.

Anchovies, bass, sardines and shellfish are all caught off the coast of Spain. But in Barcelona, sea cucumbers are a special treat.

Say it in Spanish

la casa - house
el apartamento - flat
la escuela - school
la policía - police
el periódico - newspaper
la revista - magazine
las vacaciones - holidays
la televisión - television

Trade and Industry

THE LAND OF GOLD

For many centuries, Spain has been known for its mining, food production, pottery and textiles. Today, modern machinery and technology have helped Spain to develop manufacturing and food processing industries.

The Arabs, who conquered the country in the 7th century, called Spain *El Dorado* (the land of gold). This is because the Iberians, the first people to live in Spain, mined gold and silver. Spain now mines coal and iron in the north.

Over the last 30 years, Spain has made most of its money from tourism. This money has been used to develop industry. Spain is one of the largest car manufacturers in the world and exports more cars than any other Western European country.

Spain also exports a lot of textiles, including woollen cloth. Merino sheep, known all over the world for their long, soft wool, were first bred in Spain. There is now a growing clothing industry, with fashion houses in Madrid and Barcelona.

THE FOOD FACTORY

The Romans used Spain to produce food for Italy, and Spain has been exporting food ever since. Canned fruit and fish, bottled wines and sherries, and olive oil are sold all over the world. Fresh fruit is also exported. Tomatoes and strawberries are grown, using the most modern methods, to produce early crops for northern Europe.

Cork is made from the bark of the cork oak tree which is grown all over southern Spain.

Sweet-smelling oranges are not only eaten or made into juice and jam. Their aromatic oils are also used in perfumes and soaps.

Say it in Spanish
el oro - gold
la lana - wool
el cuero - leather
la fábrica - factory
los vestidos - clothes
el corcho - cork
la naranja - orange

THE EUROPEAN COMMUNITY

Spain joined the European Community (EC) in 1985, and became a full member in 1992. The EC has helped Spain by giving money to develop the poorer regions. But membership of the EC has also caused a lot of unemployment in Spain.

Spanish Oranges

YOU WILL NEED:

TAPE

MEDIUM-SIZED PAPER BAG

A LENGTH OF RIBBON ABOUT THE SAME WIDTH AS THE TAPE

TOOTHPICK

1 FRESH FIRM ORANGE

CLOVES

2 TEASPOONS OF GROUND CINNAMON

1 TABLESPOON OF ORRIS ROOT POWDER (AVAILABLE FROM SPECIALTY FRAGRANCE OR HEALTH FOOD STORES)

One of the easiest ways to preserve and enjoy the delicious smell of an orange is to make an orange pomander.

1. Fasten the sticky tape around the orange as shown.

A word of warning - orange pomanders take about five weeks to dry out properly, so be patient!

2. Pierce the orange skin with the cocktail stick and push a clove, pointed end first, into the hole. Cover all four sections of the orange with cloves in the same way.

3. Tip the cinnamon and orris root powder into the paper bag. Shake the bag to mix the two powders together. Drop in the orange and continue shaking the bag until the orange is completely covered with the mixture. (The orris root powder will help the scent of the orange and cinnamon last longer.)

4. Leave the orange, in its bag, in a warm, dry place for about five weeks.

5. After this time, take the orange out of the bag. Blow away the excess powder and remove the sticky tape. Tie the ribbon along the rows left by the tape and hang your pomander in your wardrobe. It will make your clothes smell wonderfully fruity ... and ward off hungry moths.

Sport

Spain was the host for the 1992 Barcelona Olympic Games. It also won many medals, proving that Spain is becoming a powerful sporting nation with stars in many sports.

FAMOUS NAMES

Tennis has become a popular sport in Spain, thanks to the success of the Sanchez family. Severiano Ballasteros has made golf very popular because of his own success at the game. There are numerous golf courses throughout Spain.

At the Barcelona Olympics, Prince Felipe, the son of King Juan Carlos, represented Spain in yachting.

JUST FOOTBALL?

Football teams such as Réal Madrid, Barcelona and Atlético Bilbao are famous throughout the world. They attract thousands of supporters. But the teams represent more than just a game. During the rule of General Franco, people were not allowed to hold political meetings. The Basques, Catalonians and Galicians were not encouraged to develop their separate cultures and languages. So football teams were the symbols of the regions and gave supporters the chance to get together and show pride in their cultures.

FUN AND GAMES

In the Basque region, a unique game known as *jai alai*, or *pelota vasca* is played. It is a fast ball game played in a walled concrete court. The ball is hurled against the wall with the bare hand or with basketwork rackets.

Traffic often has to be stopped because of a road-running race or a cycling competition.

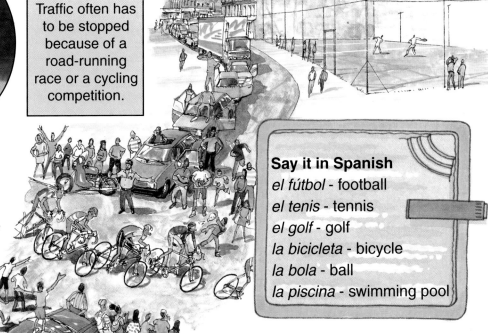

Say it in Spanish
el fútbol - football
el tenis - tennis
el golf - golf
la bicicleta - bicycle
la bola - ball
la piscina - swimming pool

Tourist Spots

Over 50 million tourists, mainly from Scandinavia, Germany, Holland, France, Britain and Portugal flock to Spain every year. Many lie on the hot, sandy beaches, or swim in the warm sea. But there are many other exciting places to visit, from mountains to monuments.

Travelling by air is very important in Spain. The three major airports are in Madrid, Palma de Mallorca and Barcelona. Iberia is one of Spain's national airlines.

GETTING AROUND

Spain has had to build many new roads in order to keep pace with its development.

The railways have also been modernized. A brand new train, *Ave* (The Bird), now travels from Madrid to Seville in only three hours. This helps to make all parts of Spain accessible to tourists.

THE CONCRETE COAST

Many tourists head for the resorts between the Costa Brava in the north and the Costa del Sol in the south. High-rise hotels, cafes, restaurants and nightclubs line the coast. Here, the tourist industry provides jobs for hundreds of thousands of Spanish workers.

But there are also quieter, less well known areas to stay in. The Costa de la Luz in the south, near Portugal, and the rocky coastline of Galicia and Asturias in the north, are still unspoilt by the tourist industry.

WINTER IN THE SUN

One of the most popular skiing centres is Navacerrada, which lies to the north of Madrid in the Guadarrama mountains. Skiing holidays are often cheaper in Spain than in France, Austria and Switzerland.

One of the best known resorts in the Balearic Islands is Mallorca. Some resorts in the Canary Islands, however, have been so taken over by tourism that they have lost their Spanish character. Resorts such as Tenerife (*below*) have become very international.

HUNTING DOWN HISTORY

There is much to see in Spain which reflects the country's rich past. For many centuries, pilgrims have made their way to the Cathedral of Santiago de Compostela in Galicia. Here, the remains of the Apostle of St. James are thought to be contained. It is the second most important shrine to Catholics after Saint Peter's Cathedral in Rome.

There are magnificent castles, such as Calatrava and Siguenza in Castile-La-Mancha. Another attraction is the Great Mosque in Córdoba and the prayer tower in Seville, examples of exotic Arab architecture.

Torre del Oro, Seville

Say it in Spanish
el hotel - hotel
el restaurante - restaurant
esquiar - skiing
la catedral - cathedral
ferrocarril - railway

The Arts

Spain is a country with such a rich mixture of peoples and traditions that there is great variety in its art, music and literature.

El Greco (1541-1614)
A painter of fine religious works with a very intense and personal style.

Francisco Goya (1746-1828)
An 18th century artist who surprised the art world with his pictures of bullfights and political scenes. He was also very skilled as a portrait painter.

Pablo Picasso (1881-1973)
Probably the most famous Spanish artist. He began the style of painting known as Cubism. Picasso's best known work is probably *Guernica* which shows the horror of the bombing of this Spanish town in 1937.

Salvador Dali (1904-1989)
Another very famous painter whose paintings do not look like real life. This style of painting *(left)* is called Surrealism.

A WAY WITH WORDS

The most famous Spanish book is *Don Quixote*, written in 1605 by Miguel de Cervantes (1547-1616). Millions of copies of this book have been sold throughout the world.

Spain has produced a mass of great literature, from Arabic and Jewish poetry written in the 10th century, to the poetry and plays written in the 1920s by Frederico García Lorca (1898-1936).

Modern day writers include Camilo José Cela (b. 1916) who won the Nobel Prize for Literature in 1989. His best known work is probably *The Beehive*.

FOLK DANCES AND MUSIC

Spaniards are very proud of their traditional folk music which varies from region to region. In Barcelona, you can see street musicians playing a type of oboe, a horn, a recorder or a little drum. Folk songs in Madrid are performed to the sound of an accordion. Musicians in the Basque region play a special three-holed oboe, called a *txitsu*, and in Asturia, people dance to a *gaita*, or a small bagpipe.

The national dance of Catalonia is the *sardana*, a sedate dance which probably originated in Greece.

A sword dance is still performed by men in Galicia, who dance to music played on small bagpipes.

FLAMENCO!

Spain is famous for its centuries-old Andalucían flamenco. Flamenco is thought of as a dance, but it is really music performed by a singer and a guitarist. Flamenco is a mixture of many different styles of music. The guitar music sounds dramatic and the brightly coloured dancers often look happy, but the songs are nearly always sad love stories. Many dancers go to professional flamenco dance schools to learn their art.

Say it in Spanish
el artista - artist
la pintura - painting
el autor - author
el libro - book
la musica - music
la guitarra - guitar
el bailador - dance

Flamenco Fever!

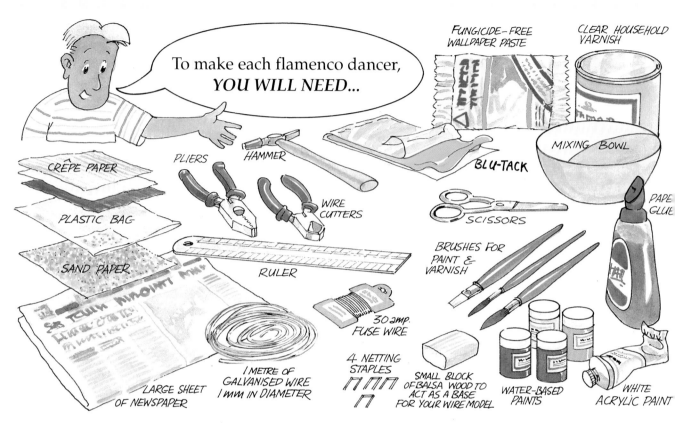

To make each flamenco dancer, **YOU WILL NEED...**

CRÊPE PAPER

PLASTIC BAG

SAND PAPER

PLIERS

HAMMER

WIRE CUTTERS

RULER

LARGE SHEET OF NEWSPAPER

I METRE OF GALVANISED WIRE I MM IN DIAMETER

30 amp. FUSE WIRE

4 NETTING STAPLES

SMALL BLOCK OF BALSA WOOD TO ACT AS A BASE FOR YOUR WIRE MODEL

FUNGICIDE-FREE WALLPAPER PASTE

CLEAR HOUSEHOLD VARNISH

BLU-TACK

MIXING BOWL

SCISSORS

BRUSHES FOR PAINT & VARNISH

PAPER GLUE

WATER-BASED PAINTS

WHITE ACRYLIC PAINT

If you get the chance to see flamenco dancers in action, watch them carefully and then try to recreate their poses when you make these models.

Ask an adult to help you.

1. Cut the wire into three equal lengths. Use the pliers to bend one end of one of these lengths, to make the shape of a foot. Secure the foot to the wood base with two staples. Be careful not to poke your eye with wire!

2. Loop the top of the wire into a head and twist it around to form the neck.

22

3. To make the arms, twist a length of wire around the neck and fix it in place with the pliers. If the arms won't stay still, secure them with blu-tack.

4. Loop the ends of the arms into hands and bend the arms into a flamenco pose.

5. Bend one end of the remaining length of wire into a foot and secure it to the base as before.

(Make sure that the feet and legs are in the right position to support your model.)

6. Wind the leg around the trunk of your model and secure the end of it to the arms.

7. Cut the fuse wire into lengths approximately 15 cm long, and twist them round your model to give it more shape. If your model has any sharp edges, cut them off with the pliers.

To make papier mâché

8. Tear the newspaper into tiny strips. Put the strips into the bowl, cover them with hot water and leave them to soak for at least 12 hours.

9. Drain the water from the bowl and squeeze the paper in your hands as hard as you can to get rid of the excess water. Put the paper in the bowl again and mix in enough wallpaper paste to make a spongy pulp.

23

10. Squeeze a layer of pulp over your model and then add curves and bumps where needed. Put any leftover papier mâché in a sealed plastic bag and store it in a cool damp place.

11. When your model is complete, carefully remove the staples with the pliers. Then lay your model down gently and cover its feet with papier mâché. Make sure that the base of the feet are flat and that your model can stand.

12. Leave your model in a warm place to dry. This will probably take about three days. Check it occasionally as it dries to make sure that it can still stand up. If it doesn't, carefully reposition its legs.

13. When your model is dry, fill in any cracks with the leftover papier mâché. Wait for this to dry and then rub the whole model with sandpaper to make it smooth.

14. Before you paint any details, cover your model with a coat of white acrylic paint. This will help to cover up the newsprint.

15. When the undercoat is dry, start adding painted details. When these are dry, paint your model with a coat of varnish.

To make a frilly flamenco skirt

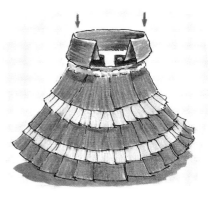

16. Cut out a circle of crêpe paper as shown. The smaller circle needs to be big enough to fit around your model's hips.

17. Dab some glue around the bottom of the skirt and fold a strip of crêpe paper onto it. Add more frills in the same way.

18. To finish, glue a paper waistband onto the skirt. Then glue the waist band onto your model and stick the back of the skirt together.

If your dancer refuses to stand, stick some blu-tack under his or her feet.

Festivals

Holidays, festivals and fun are often linked with holy days in Spain. But in many towns and villages people also celebrate their harvests of wheat, wine or even fish. Some of Spain's most colourful festivals take place during Holy Week or Easter. The festivals are great fun and are usually celebrated out in the streets.

FEASTING

Most festivals are celebrated with processions, dancing and eating specially prepared feasts. One of the two major festivals is Corpus Christi, on the second Thursday after Whitsun. The other is Assumption on 15 August. Southern Spain celebrates this with parades of bright costumes and statues, flamenco and *turrón* stalls.

HOLIDAYS FOR ALL

Public holidays are at Christmas, Easter and the New Year. May Day, too, is a day's holiday for all workers. There are also other national holidays, such as All Saint's Day and Columbus' Day, which is celebrated on October 12th when Columbus set sail for America 500 years ago. Almost every village celebrates its own saint's day as well.

Imagine a festival called "The Burial of the Sardine!" It is celebrated at the end of Lent in Murcia. Singing, dancing and processions are followed by fireworks and the solemn burning of a single sardine.

In Valencia, on 19 March, people celebrate the *Fallas de San José*. The festival began many centuries ago when carpenters burned wood chips and shavings on Saint Joseph's Day. Not only did this mark the Saint's day, but also the end of winter and the beginning of spring.

Today, enormous statues of wax, wood and plaster are paraded through the streets. After five days of fireworks and feasting, the statues are burned.

Pamplona's famous bull-running festival takes place on Saint Fermin's day in July.

Valencia's tomato-throwing festival celebrates the region's huge, juicy tomatoes.

Say it in Spanish
la fiesta - holiday
el toro - bull
la Natividád - Christmas
la Pascua - Easter
el Año Nuevo - New Year
los fuegos artificiales - fireworks

Spanish History

From dinosaurs and dolmens to castles and kings, Spain's rich history can be seen in every region.

THE FIRST IBERIANS

Paintings in the Altamira caves in northern Spain are thought to be about 12,000 years old. They show life in Iberia, the vast piece of land that includes Spain and Portugal. The first Iberians were joined in about 3,000 BC by North Africans. These peoples developed a very rich culture.

THE BATTLE FOR SPAIN

People from many parts of Europe and the Middle East realised that Iberia was an area full of wealth. The first Iberians were soon joined by settlements of Greeks, Phoenicians, Jews, Celts and Carthaginians.

ROMAN RULE

By 206 BC, the mighty Roman army had surged through Iberia. The Romans built great cities, long roads, bridges and aqueducts. Above all, they brought their language, which spread throughout the land. But the Roman army became too big to manage. Visigoths swept down from northern Europe, followed by Arabs from North Africa.

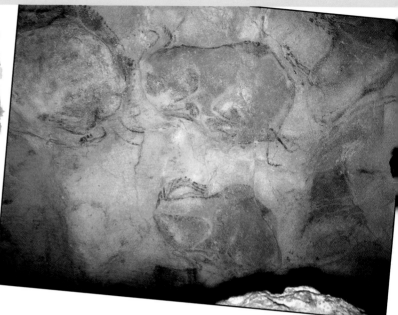

IBERIA AND ISLAM

The Arabs brought with them a new religion, Islam. They built splendid cities, and beautiful mosques and gardens. With the Jewish communities, they developed music, science, mathematics, medicine and even surgery.

THE CHRISTIAN MONARCHS

But Christians from the north of Iberia gradually conquered the Muslims. In 1469, Spain became united under the Catholic monarchs when Queen Isabella of Castile and King Ferdinand of Aragon married. For a hundred years, Spain was rich and powerful. But by the end of the 16th century, the country was in decay. Right up to the 20th century, Spain was poor and disorganised. But Spain survived war and dictatorship until 1975, when King Juan Carlos took the throne. Spain is now a flourishing democratic monarchy.

People of the Past

EL CID

El Cid was the greatest Christian general, who conquered Castile-Léon in the 11th century.

CHRISTOPHER COLUMBUS

In 1492, Christopher Columbus set sail for America.

GENERAL FRANCO

General Franco ruled Spain for 30 years as a dictatorship. When he died in 1975, King Juan Carlos was named as his successor. But the King did not take the power for himself, unlike Franco. Instead, he helped to set up a modern, democratic government.

Say it in Spanish:
el rey - king
la raina - queen
la historia - history
la batalla - battle

TIME BAND

206 BC Iberia under the Roman Empire

711 AD Arab rule begins in Spain

1469 Spain becomes a monarchy following the marriage of Ferdinand of Aragon and Isabella of Castille

1618 - 1648 Spain takes part in the Thirty Years' War on the side of the Austrian Hapsburgs

1640 Portugal separates from Spain

1873 First Republic established by the Cortes

1874 End of the First Republic

1878 Spanish - American War - Spain loses

1914 - 1918 World War 1 - Spain remains neutral

1923 General Primo de Rivera becomes dictator and gets rid of the Cortes

1930 Primo de Rivera resigns

1931 Beginning of Second Republic, bringing equality to women and the poor

1936 - 1939 Spanish Civil War - Franco becomes dictator

1939 - 1945 World War 11 - Spain remains neutral

1975 Franco dies - democracy begins

Picture Pairs

Play Picture Pairs and see how many of the Spanish words in this book you actually remember! The instructions given here are for two to four players, but as your Spanish vocabulary increases, you might like to make more cards and include more players.

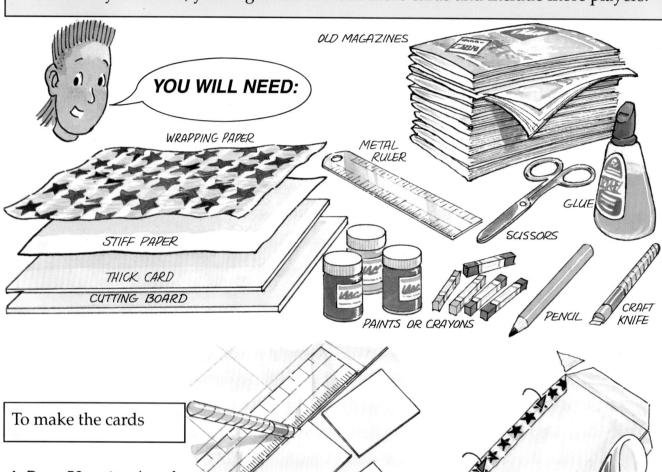

YOU WILL NEED:

OLD MAGAZINES

WRAPPING PAPER

METAL RULER

STIFF PAPER

THICK CARD

CUTTING BOARD

PAINTS OR CRAYONS

SCISSORS

GLUE

PENCIL

CRAFT KNIFE

To make the cards

1. Draw 50 rectangles of the same size onto the card and carefully cut them out using the craft knife

2. Draw another 50 rectangles onto the wrapping paper and cut them out too. These rectangles should be about 2 cm longer and wider than the card ones.

3. Cut the corners of the paper rectangles as shown and glue them onto your cards.

4. Draw 25 rectangles, slightly smaller than your cards onto the stiff paper and cut them out.

5. Choose 25 Spanish words from this book and write them down with their English translations. Keep this list beside you when you play the game.

6. Look through the magazines and cut out any photographs which illustrate the words you have chosen. If you can't find suitable pictures, cut out some more rectangles from stiff paper and paint pictures of your words on them.

7. Stick each photograph or picture onto the front of one of your cards. Glue the stiff paper rectangles onto the rest of the pack and write a Spanish word from your list on each one.

To play the game
The object of Picture Pairs is to collect pairs of cards made up of words and their matching picture.

Each player starts the game with seven cards. The rest of the pack is placed face down on the table. If you have any pairs, put them on the table in front of you.

Then ask one of the other players if he/she has a card that you need to make a pair. If that player has the card requested, he/she must hand it over and you win the pair and have another turn. If he/she does not have the card, you take a card from the pack in the middle and the turn passes to the next person.

All word cards must be translated into English. If you cannot remember the translation of a word, look it up and miss your next go.

The player who pairs all his/her cards first is the winner.

31

Index